Publishers

A SHORT GUIDE TO:
DATING, COURTSHIP & MARRIAGE

YAA OBUO-DADZIE

ISBN NO: 978-0-9575824-0-8

PRINTED IN THE UNITED KINGDOM
PRINTED BY: IMPRINTS ACADEMIC LTD, EXETER
COVER DESIGN BY **OMEGAHAUSE MULTIMEDIA**

Published by: G.Y.N.S.O.D

DEDICATION

This book is dedicated to God Almighty first and foremost for His wisdom and guidance. To my beloved parents, who did not know I was writing this book; Rev. Kwabena & Mrs .Elizabeth Obuo-Dadzie; and Ms. Margaret Sarpong-Kwakwa, who has taught me all I need to know about a Christian home and marriage.

To my two wonderful grandmothers Ms. Esther Ofori and Mrs. Esther Afrakoma Amofa

To my beloved sisters, their husbands and their children; Ms. Pearl Dadzie; Mr. Kenneth & Mrs Ruby Annobil-Brew; Fiona Mensah & Chris Shomulu; Lucy Asafo; Eva & Glen Conway; David & Priscilla Okai; Jenifer & Kwaku Kwaning; Abigail Owusu-Sekyere; Dr. Leslie & Dr. Mrs MaryAnn Quarcopome. To my big brother, advisor, counsellor and friend Kwaku Owusu Acheampong; To my brother and twin Nana Kwame Osei-Tutu. Not forgetting my god-sons Master Andrew-Sampson Berko-Boateng and Master Elijah Glen Conway.

To my uncles and aunties: Ms. Juliet Sarpong-Kwakwa, Mrs. Josephine Boateng; Mr. Frank & Mrs. Benita Akoto; Ms. Gloria Sarpong-Kwakwa; Mr. Justin & Mrs .Ladwan Berko-Boateng; Mrs.Eva Opoku; Rev Daniel Darko; Rev. Prophetess Sarah & Mr. George Mensah; Rev. Allen & Mrs. Gloria Opoku; To my aunties, uncles, cousins, the entire Sarpong-Kwakwa and Dadzie families worldwide.

To my mentor, teacher, motivator (and his wife) Mr. Eric & Mrs .Saskia Appiah (Eric Reverence) . To Pastor and Mrs. Osei Boafo (OSBY, FCI) for your support and advice.

To all my girlfriends, my pillars, who have used me as a counsellor through the years to write this book. This book's to you; Mr. & Mrs. Mensah (Joe & Kenisha);Yetunde Afolabi; Mr. & Mrs. Kalu(Nnana and Claire); Khadija Kande; Racheal Akiteng; Melisa Caramba-Coker; Samia Ali and Abigail Akindiya.

To my two best male friends in the world, we fight, we argue, but we still love each other and support ourselves through prayers and advice: Fadi Muanga and Samuel Kwame Osei-Yeboah.

A SHORT GUIDE TO:
Dating, Courtship & Marriage
is dedicated to everyone who will buy and read it.

ACKNOWLEDGEMENT

I would like to express my deep gratitude to God Almighty for the insight and wisdom to write this book.

What can I do without these two pillars in my life: my parents: Rev. Kwabena Mensah Fodjour & Mrs Elizabeth Akua Asantewaa Obuo Dadzie for being role models and demonstrating the way relationships have to be nurtured and for keeping to high standards in their everyday lives at home.

My sincere appreciation goes to Minister Eric Appiah (Eric Reverence) for nagging me and all his complains which has finally produced this book. To Pastor Osei-Boafo (OSBY) for his help, contribution, suggestions and advice.

To my Uncle, Rev. Daniel Darko for all his reading time, contributions and for keeping the surprise.

My sincere acknowledgement to Omegahouse Multimedia (Joe Baidoo & Edem Caliph) for the cover design and re-arrangement of text.

CONTENT

PREFACE:

With the rate of divorce so high, we cannot afford to sit on the sidelines and do nothing about it.

This book contains all you need to know before you decide to date. It contains what you should learn and how- to pick up signals from your partners to provide you with a successful marriage. The book gives advice to singles, separated folks, and married or divorced people, with the aim of helping them break free from the stress of relationships.

The book is for all ages, teenagers, adults, everyone. It also provides a classic knowledge of understanding the opposite sex. It looks at things such as the different love and apology languages, which can be unique to every individual. This book helps couples to know their different communication styles and how-to use them to build a happy relationship.

The book talks about the basic ingredients needed for every relationship or marriage. Ingredients like love, communication, commitment, trust, and so on. All are explained in great detail in this book. This book also explains how these elements can be implemented and put into place.

The book also discusses high divorce rates and how-to divorce proof your marriage.

It looks at marriage in this 21st century where both husbands and wives are bread- winners of the family.

I believe this book is a short introduction, but it will be a blessing to anyone who reads it.

This book will enlighten you and give you a deeper understanding of the meaning of marriage. Happy reading!

Daughters of Jerusalem, I charge you: do not arouse or awaken love until it desires.

'Songs of Solomon 8:4'....

CHAPTER 1
BEFORE DATING

BEFORE DATING:

Singleness must be seen as a blessing and an opportunity to develop one's self. There is a reason for being single. This is the time you take out to pray for signs that will help you to recognise the right one. When Abraham was getting old and about to die, he sent his senior servant to seek a wife for his son Isaac. He prayed for a sign.

Genesis 24:12-23

[12] Then he prayed, "LORD, God of my master Abraham, make me successful today, and show kindness to my master Abraham. [13] See, I am standing beside this spring, and the daughters of the townspeople are coming out to draw water. [14] May it be that when I say to a young woman, 'Please let down your jar that I may have a drink,' and she says, 'Drink, and I'll water your camels too'—let her be the one you have chosen for your servant Isaac. By this I will know that you have shown kindness to my master.

"[15] Before he had finished praying, Rebekah came out with her jar on her shoulder. She was the daughter of Bethuel son of Milkah, who was the wife of Abraham's brother Nahor. [16] The

woman was very beautiful, a virgin; no man had ever slept with her. She went down to the spring, filled her jar and came up again. [17] The servant hurried to meet her and said, "Please give me a little water from your jar." [18] "Drink, my lord," she said, and quickly lowered the jar to her hands and gave him a drink. [19] after she had given him a drink, she said, "I'll draw water for your camels too, until they have had enough to drink." [20] So she quickly emptied her jar into the trough, ran back to the well to draw more water, and drew enough for all his camels.

[21] Without saying a word, the man watched her closely to learn whether or not the LORD had made his journey successful. [22] when the camels had finished drinking, the man took out a gold nose ring weighing a beka and two gold bracelets weighing ten shekels. [23] Then he asked, "Whose daughter are you? Please tell me, is there room in your father's house for us to spend the night?"

There is a lot of confusion about whether dating and courtship are the same and if they are important. Most people classify it as one thing, where others put in into two different categories. This can be understandable based on the experience of the person. Some people, on the other hand, do not believe in dating and courtship because they believe others can pretend during the process. Before dating, there are a few things an individual has to be aware of or put into place before embarking on the journey. Before you decide to date, there are things you must be sure you know about.

You must have:

- An intimate relationship with God
- Self-worth and value
- Self-esteem
- Be confident
- Be emotionally stable
- Be a whole person
- Be dependent on your own abilities
- Have a vision and know what you want in life
- Finally, you must know a relationship is an added blessing, not a reliability and a bonus to your life

CHAPTER 2
DATING

DATING:

There are different definitions to dating. Most people can define it in their own words depending on their experiences. Dating simply can be defined as the friendship between two people, with an idea of studying each other through activities in life to assess their suitability as a life partner or for an intimate relationship. Activities like going out for a meal, movies, etc., can build the relationship.

Before dating one must be sure they are ready to date, have dated *oneself* in the sense that they are confident and know what they want; know what they expect from the dating experience, and be ready to accept what the experience will/may bring.

The dating period may take between two to four weeks before it can continue to the next stage: courtship; but this timeframe also may vary depending on the persons involved. Before dating continues to courtship, the two people must agree to be in the relationship. Do not leave someone guessing after a date whether you would want to be in a relationship with them or not, especially if you like them. It is heartening and sometimes stressful when that happens to the person involved. It helps to prevent wasting time, when each individual knows where they stand so they can move on.

• REASONS FOR DATING:

The reason why some people date is to fulfil a self-worth, because they are empty and they think they need someone in their lives to complete the puzzle. This is the greatest mistake since there seems to be an expectation that needs to be met. Do not be in a relationship because you feel you need someone financially to assist you, someone to quench your sexual desires or just for the fun of it.

The first step of dating should be building a friendship. In order to have a successful relationship, the person you are dating must be your friend; that relationship needs to be established. He or she needs to be a friend you can talk to, confide in, play with, trust and share your inner secrets with.

To avoid wasting time, you must observe this person you want to date from afar, do some research on them, and investigate them. You need to make sure the person is somebody you can relate to or be with, before deciding to have any connection with them. When this is done, it makes it easier to avoid disappointments later on in the relationship, with each other saying, 'We have wasted each other's time. '

The first motivation   for getting into a relationship should be one that you know can lead to courtship or marriage, or else you will both waste each other's time. It is advised that relationships or dating should graduate to courtship, if the sole purpose of it is that it will lead to marriage. It is also advised that courtship should not be too long to avoid any sexual immorality.

CHAPTER 3
COURTSHIP

COURTSHIP:

This is the time when you get to know each order better before proceeding to the next level and extending it to the outside world. When this is done, it makes it easier to know if both of you are suitable for each other. During courtship there are habits, attitudes, likes and dislikes that come up.

This is the time to find a good way to talk about them. Do not feel bad or strange to talk about them. After all, good and bad habits will continue into the marriage and may cause major problems ahead.

Some of these habits and attitudes or behaviours can be changed, compromised and others cannot. It takes prayer to change those attitudes and behaviours. Do not ever think you can do it on your own. Sometimes it takes sacrifice, pampering and going the extra mile to see the change happen.

There are also important habits that need to be in place during the courting and dating period. It is difficult for most couples who are married these days to pray in their marriage.

Prayer and reading the word should be initiated if you are both Christians, as the fundamental source of your dating and courting period.

It is always and rightly said that 'A couple who prays together, stays together.' The couple who are able to kneel before God together are lifted together and go through many trials together.

It can be hard or difficult in these modern times, especially when you may not be living together, or may be working different shifts and are busy. It does not have to be an hour-long prayer, or two hours prayers; it does not have to be at a particular time or place, or even both of you together.

You can even pray over the phone; it is still called prayer and reading the word. Always remember where two or three are gathered in His name, when both set their hearts, your heart on a topic to pray over, it will do wonders in your relationship before the marriage, says the Lord.

One thing each person should know is no one is perfect, but everyone can be lived with. You must be with the person you want to be with.

Relationships can be demanding and it can be a full-time job; do not go into it if you are not ready. If you both understand each other and learn to solve your problems amicably knowing no one is perfect, then it will be greatest experience of your lives.

Through the knowing of each other, love grows. Love does not grow just within a second of knowing or seeing someone. Do not rush to say the words 'I love you' because later on in the courtship you will find things that will annoy you to the brim and may even turn you off to that person.

Loves grows through friendship, sharing time and getting to know each other. This process can take days to weeks, months to years. It is a gradual process. It cannot happen in a second or a minute. It takes time and patience.

The first instance you saw a person and liked the person, and wished you could be in their lives, does not mean you love them.

It's called infatuation. Infatuation, according to some dictionaries, is the state of being completely carried away by unreasoned passion or love; been attracted or having some form of addictive love for a person. Normally this is a short-lived passion or admiration for the person.

Other dictionaries define it as a foolish and usually extravagant passion or love or admiration. Spending time with the person will help you define what you are feeling, whether it is infatuation or love.

Love is being with a person, spending time, knowing their flaws and yet still been able to boldly say 'I love you' no matter what. The bible gives clear definition of love in

1Corinthians 13:4-6 Love is patient, love is kind. It does not envy, it does not boast, it is not proud. ⁵It does not dishonour others, it is not self-seeking, it is not easily angered, it keeps no record of wrongs. ⁶Love does not delight in evil but rejoices with the truth. ⁷It always protects, always trusts, always hopes, always perseveres.

Love is not lust, or wishing to be intimate with someone without knowing them. The bible speaks and stands against it,

Galatians 5:16-26. ¹⁶So I say, walk by the Spirit, and you will not gratify the desires of the flesh. ¹⁷for the flesh desires what is contrary to the Spirit, and the Spirit what is contrary to the flesh. They are in conflict with each other, so that you are not to do whatever you want.

¹⁸But if you are led by the Spirit, you are not under the law.¹⁹The acts of the flesh are obvious: sexual immorality, impurity and debauchery; ²⁰idolatry and witchcraft; hatred, discord, jealousy, fits of rage, selfish ambition, dissensions, factions

²¹and envy; drunkenness, orgies, and the like. I warn you, as I did before, that those who live like this will not inherit the kingdom of God. ²²But the fruit of the Spirit is love, joy, peace, forbearance, kindness, goodness, faithfulness, ²³

eness and self-control. Against such things *is no law.* [24] *Those who belong to Christ Jesus have crucified the flesh with its passions and desires.* [25] *since we live by the Spirit let us keep in step with the Spirit.* [26] *Let us not become conceited, provoking and envying each other.*

Through the courtship you should know each other's vision, future and be able to share ideas. You must find out if both of you share the same views on future dreams, aspirations, religious views, family morals, marriage, children's upbringing and so on.

In reality, this will all come up when you both decide to settle down or get married.

The mistake most people make is to marry people who do not have the same aspirations in life as them, but only find out after they are married. You must have a common ground of interest, at least on some things. The other areas can be worked on.

Do not think because you love the person, knows their flaws, the person will change to support your aspirations no matter what when you get married.

Once again, people do not change when they get married. You both must have the notion you are getting married to support each other's dreams, to push each other to the top, to be each other's hero and to support each other's dreams.

Do not marry someone who does not share your dreams or will push you to the limit. That is why it is very important to be a whole person.

You must first have your self-esteem and values before you decide to date or continue your relationship to courtship or even the marriage level.

You must work on yourself. If any of this happens or your intended does not support or understand you through the process, then you always have something to fall back on.

CHAPTER 4
THE LOVE LANGUAGE

THE LOVE LANGUAGES

Most relationships are not a success due to partners not knowing what their partners need. Every relationship needs basic ingredients to survive, just as humans need air, water and food to survive each day.

This includes love, trust and security. These three things work hand in hand.

You should always treat your relationship like a plant you are looking after to bear fruit. . Once you have planted it, it would need to watered, looked after, and pruned to remove every weed or pest.

These tasks must be done in order to make it grow healthy and happy and to bear you the flower or fruits you look forward to. Without doing these things, your plant or flower will likely die.

Another good example is when you own a car, you will have to fuel it and service it, too. That is how you should always look at your relationship and treat it with care. We all have ways we would like to be loved or feel loved. This can be called our love language. Love language can be defined as the way an individual would like to be loved. For example, things and ways that can make them feel appreciated, special, whether with words or actions, whichever appeals to them most.

Courtship is also made for the love languages to be learned and studied about each other. Men, this is the only chance you can learn what your woman loves, what makes her feel like a woman, what makes her feel special and loved.

Women, this is time to know what makes your man feel like the man he is, and the things you can do to make him love you more. These are special things that will make him feel and know you are the one and only.

Rooley, a love expert ad psychologist, said "The best present a man can give his woman is his time and attention. Funny enough that is what appeals to most women, but most men see this as a woman been an attention seeker. Often, simple attention is what makes her happy, feel special and grow to love you more.

There is another saying that goes "To love a woman, never try to understand her, her feelings, what she wants you to do to make her feel special, just love her." That is the way women were created; to be understood.

That is why God made man sleep and took a bone out of him to make a woman. The meaning is only simple; just love her as you love yourself.

We can never understand why God did not mould another human out of clay. He could have done that easily. Instead, he caused Adam to fall into a deep sleep again, and took a rib to create Eve's body and bring her to life.

Women were created as receivers. Whatever you give a woman she will nurture and give it back. It is like conception, you give a woman your sperm, and she nurtures it for nine months and brings out a wonderful new life. If you do not give your woman any love or understanding, do not expect anything back. All you should and can expect back is nagging, complaining, bitterness and hurt.

And that will cause problems in the relationship. Just listen to her and understand what she communicates to you that make her happy. Some may say this sounds silly and stupid.

Women are the most complex creatures on earth, and the last thing God created; he rested after that.

Have you ever thought why that is? Why didn't God create women first? After all, he said they will be man's helpers so he could have created women first.

I believe this is because of the complexness associated with women. . The complex things that women go through monthly even cannot be understood; hormonal changes and the like. It takes divinity to understand a woman.

Sometimes to find out your partner's love language, you must learn to listen to them; hear their complaints and watch out for the signals they give you.

Importantly, you must learn to observe. Sometimes you would have to ask questions to find out what their primary love language is.

Everyone has a primary love language. It takes time to know and learn what they are. One love expert, counsellor and teacher on relationships and marriage, Gary Chapman, categorises love language into five types. The love languages include:

- **Act of spending time**- *Most people with this language as their primary love language prefer to spend time with their* partners. So, no matter what you do for them, the gifts you buy them, they will still complain because their basic and primary love language is not being met. Sometimes it is not spending the whole day with them, but just 10 minutes out of your busy schedule means a lot to them. It makes them feel special and loved. This primary love language is popular with most women. They normally say it's the presence of their partners that matters.

- **Words of affirmation**- Words of affirmation can be words of encouragement, advice and the act of being there and listening, noticing their appearance and saying something about it. It's important to say, "I love you' or 'I miss you." It also includes, "You look great today honey," "I liked what you wore today." After a bad day at work, it includes "Darling, everything will be just fine." A person with this as their primary love language will love to hear these words and phrases often in order to feel special and loved, especially with an "I love you," every morning and night. You'll be surprised how your relationship will flourish.

- **Acts of service**- This type of love language is seen mostly in men, which surprises most women as they expect physical touch to be men's primary love language. A person with act of service loves to see their partner do things for them, especially when these things are done willingly. This does not mean the person is lazy or is taking advantage of the other. This is how they were created. Particularly when married, this type of person loves to see their partner help them around the house, help them cook, clean and even surprise them with planning different occasions and anniversaries. People must be careful how they use this language because it can be abused and taken for granted.

- **Receiving gifts**- Gifts are important. A person with this as their primary love language should not and must not be seen as materialistic. This again, is mainly how they were created. Even our creator, God gave us a special gift; he continues to do so everyday of our lives, as he provides the opportunity to wake up again and live. God's gift to us makes us celebrate Christmas every year and even Easter, too. Some people have a norm where presents are to be given only on occasions like birthdays, Valentine's Day, Christmas, anniversaries, etc. Gifts or presents can be given anytime, at anywhere, whenever your heart feels like doing so. Gifts do not have to be expensive.

It can be just a handmade card, a text message during the day, a beautiful earring you saw when window shopping through the mall or a beautiful tie you think will look good on your man. This will mean a lot to the person whose primary love language is the act of receiving gifts. They will cherish them.

- **Physical touch**- Physical touch is different to lust. Some people just lust. God created intimacy for a reason, but he hates lust.

Having physical touch as a primary language does not mean lusting or always wanting to be intimate. This person with this love language likes to be hugged, cuddled, kissed and held hands when working. It can be important part of the relationship because it brings the two of you closer.

All this process does not happen in a twinkle of an eye, it takes time. It takes years, months, days and weeks. You have to be patient to know and learn them. It cannot be observed within a day or an hour.

As you date, court, spend time, pray and read the word together; it will all follow and you will both discover each other's love languages. Do not rush it if it is not happening, with time you will find and discover what your partner's love language is easily.

CHAPTER 5
THE APOLOGY LANGUAGES

THE APOLOGY LANGUAGES

Arguments, flaws are all part of our daily lives and we cannot avoid them. If they happen, how do you get your partner's love back or win their heart back. Sometimes pride does not let us apologise.

Just like their love language, they will have an apology language, too. Love experts believe we all have a particular way we would liked to be apologised to or certain words that makes us feel the person apologising means what they are saying or are truly sorry for what they have done.

You will notice through the years of dating or courting, your partner may like you to use or may like one particular way for you to apologise when they feel you have wronged them.

No matter what you do, how you apologise if they do not hear those words or see that act, they can claim you never apologised.

Hold onto that fact. That is their apology language. They can be put into five types, too.

- **Requesting forgiveness**- *People with this as their primary apology language would love to hear the words "Will you please forgive me?"*

  This does not make you the stupid one in the relationship; it makes you the wiser, the stronger and the braver.

  This also shows that you value the relationship and the person you are with. Without these words, the person with this type of language as their primary language will not be happy with any apology you give them.

- **Making restitution**- *A person with this as their primary love language would like to hear, "What can I do to make it up to you?" This makes the person with this as their apology language feel you still feel the same way about them, and you are ready to do anything to make them happy and make the relationship work.*

- *Genuinely repenting-* The entire person with this language as their primary apology language will like to hear, "I'm sorry and I will not to repeat it again or make it happen again." With these words of affirmation, it proves to the person that you have recognised your wrong doing; you are sorry and will try not to let it happen again, although you are a human.

- *Accepting responsibility-* This language can be similar to genuinely repenting. The words that mean a lot to a person with this as their primary love language is, "It's my fault," "I was wrong," "I accept the blame." If these words are not used, no matter what you say to a person with this as their primary language, they will always feel you have not apologised.

- *Expressing regret-* Expressing regret includes using words such as, "I'm sorry." Just, "I'm sorry," means a lot to a person with this as their primary apology language. This proves to the person that you are truly sorry; you have regretted what you have done.

Also, note that these words should not be abused and taken for granted in a relationship. Because you know the apology language of your partner does not mean you should continue to wrong them and abuse their apology language. Continuous usage of this will cause the relationship to break down and cause your partner to no longer trust or believe in your words.

CHAPTER 6
COUNSELLING

COUNSELLING

Another important requirement that couples must do before they get married is to have a counselling session.

Counselling also comes under the self-assessing process, and this is done with an agreement between the two persons. This session can be with their pastor or a professional marriage counsellor.

These sessions helps couples to find out deeper things about themselves through the sharing and asking of questions.

It cannot be emphasised how important counselling is before you walk down the aisle and say *I do*. It usually takes between three to six months depending on the individuals, their church, issues that crop up, etc. Questions that can be asked during this session may include family backgrounds, any health problems, and any issues that might affect or come up during the marriage.

Couples are also taught how to be good husbands and wives during the counselling period. Wedding dates and programs on the day are discussed at counselling.

This also gives the couple an opportunity to ask any questions about marriage or the wedding that they do not understand.

CHAPTER 7
MARRIAGE

MARRIAGE

During the courtship and dating, there are so many things that need to be observed and learned.

There are self-assessments; there are questions to be asked about the different things you have studied about your partner.

Questions such as: "Is this person someone I can live solely with, for the rest of my life?" and, "Am I fully prepared to commit to one person for the rest of my life?"

If your self assessment and answers ends up with a "yes," then you are ready to marry your partner. Getting married is a lifelong commitment, it is a serious business and God treats it as such.

What will be your motivations or your reasons for wanting to get married? If it is merely due to financial reasons, or due to family pressures or emotional security, then you are not ready to get married. You need to pray and search your inner self before you embark on that journey.

Get married when you want to get married, not when you feel like you should. Do not allow peer or family pressure to force you. The bible even says there is time for everything.

*Ecclesiastes 3:1-3- **There is a time for everything, and a season for every activity under the heavens:***

God sees marriage as God being married to the church and that is how he wants each and every individual to see it. He wants married couples to be selfless in marriage, sacrifice as he did when he sent his only child to die for humanity. It took only sacrifice and that is how he would like marriage to be like. God put us first, if he hadn't, he would not have sent his only son to die on the cross.

Marriage was the first thing instituted by God before sin. God instituted and ordained marriage. Marriage is not man's idea.

When God created Adam, he realised it was not good for him to live alone; so he decided to make him a helper called Eve. God put Adam to sleep and through his sleep took a rib and formed a woman out of that rib.

When Adam awakened, he saw what God had done and, indeed, it was good to his eyes.

Adam looked at the beautiful creature God has created and said to God, "This is the rib of my rib and the bone of my bone to be each other's companion."

Genesis 2:21-23- [21] *so the LORD God caused the man to fall into a deep sleep; and while he was sleeping, he took one of the man's ribs and then closed up the place with flesh.* [22] *Then the LORD God made a woman from the rib he had taken out of the man, and he brought her to the man.* [23] *The man said, "This is now bone of my bones and flesh of my flesh; she shall be called 'woman,' for she was taken out of man."* Genesis 2:18- [18] *The LORD God said, "It is not good for the man to be alone. I will make a helper suitable for him."*

The companionship God created in marriage comes with openness, being truthful with each other and not hiding things. When God created Adam and Eve, they were both naked, which symbolizes the openness God expects in marriage. God says when we become his children, he no longer treats us as servants, but as children; so he discloses whatever he wants to do to us.

Genesis 2:25- [25] *Adam and his wife were both naked, and they felt no shame.*

By doing this God is proving that both will be one body, one soul, and one spirit, one being. There are ways to be open in the relationship by letting your partner know about your past relationships, financial history, without or with debts, etc.

Another important question that should come to your mind when you have decided to marry this person is: "Do I truly trust this person?" Every successful relationship or marriage should be based on love, trust and respect. These should be the fundamental rocks, apart from God, which you both have developed about each other through the period of the dating and courtship.

Is like building a house on a solid rock, using the proper bricks and mortar to complete it; you are confident and know that no matter what storm comes through the house, the house will stand and will not fall. Without these elements it is like building a house on sand, where even a slight wind can just bring it down. To trust this person means to believe in them and to have faith in them.

Do you know at least half of his or her family members before getting married? Would you feel left out or insecure if you saw your partner talking to the opposite sex?

Most relationships and marriages break up due to a lack of trust and truthfulness. If you cannot affirm and answer these questions boldly, "I trust my partner," then do not attempt marriage.

You must deal with this and other issues before walking down that aisle or there will be trouble down the road. Marriage is the merging of two hearts, two souls and two bodies. You both have to be soul mates. If you give God the reins, He will bless your marriage.

A relationship between soul mates is often described as one that feels like it is meant to be. Soul mates have a sense of familiarity and harmony between them that brings out the best in both of them. Wilbert Donald Gough wrote, "In marriage, being the right person is as important as finding the right person."

It is also important for married couples to have a mentor in their life. This mentor is someone who has been married for a long time; someone who they can look up to; someone who can advise, pray and counsel them when there are problems in their marriage.

This person must not be seen as a solution centre where you drop all your problems. Couples must learn to solve problems between them and to refrain from allowing the outside world (even their own families) into their issues.

Through self-assessing, one must be able to answer more questions like, "Can I make someone else my first priority? Can I be faithful for the rest of my life?

Am I ready to lay my life down, as Christ did, for someone else? Can I be responsible for someone else's emotional, spiritual and physical being?"

CHAPTER 8
BASIC ELEMENTS NEEDED
FOR MARRIAGE

BASIC ELEMENTS
NEEDED FOR MARRIAGE

There are ingredients that make a successful relationship or marriage

LOVE

Some dictionaries define love as a great liking and the feeling of wanting to be with someone; the feeling of wanting to be part of their lives.

It can be said as the feeling of wanting to hear from a person or see them mostly, and being greatly concerned about their well-being and life; what goes in and out of their lives. Love is not being selfish, but wanting to share what you have with others.

The bible gives clear definitions of what love is 1 Corinthians 13:4- [4] Love is patient, love is kind. It does not envy, it does not boast, it is not proud. [5] It does not dishonour others, it is not self-seeking, it is not easily angered, and it keeps no record of wrongs. [6] Love does not delight in evil but rejoices with the truth. [7] It always protects, always trusts, always hopes, always perseveres

To love, you have to be understanding, and be able to put your needs last. Your "I" in your relationship and statements must turn to "you." Jerry McCant wrote, "You can never be happily married to another until you get a divorce from yourself."

A successful marriage demands a certain death of self. Love does not want to be intimate with the person straight away. It takes time to learn and understand the needs and wants of the other person.

You feel in love when every time you see this person you catch your breath, your heart pounds, skips a beat and your palms start to sweat. True love is selfless; taking each other for granted is not love. Love is not selfish.

Philippians 2:3- Do nothing out of selfish ambition or vain conceit. Rather, in humility value others above yourselves

Most people treat strangers better than they treat their husbands and wives. Love must be sincere.

Romans 12:9 [9] Love must be sincere. Hate what is evil; cling to what is good.

It is impossible to be sincere if you are always saying what you think your partner wants to hear. Love gives and it is therefore rewarded. God rewarded Adam with Eve, a helpmate; Eve with Adam to provide her with love and security.

If your woman feels unsecured and not loved in the relationship, then you must question yourself and ask God for guidance.

1 Corinthians 13:7- love always protects, always trusts, always hopes, always perseveres.

There are types of love but there are three important ones that needs to demonstrated in marriages: **Agape, Phileo and Eros**

> 1. **Agape** - *This love sees beyond everything. It is the love that is able to love the other person no matter what the other is like, in spite of their flaws. This is the kind of love God demonstrates to us in Romans 5:8——[8] but God demonstrates his own love for us in this: While we were still sinners, Christ died*

for us. He would like to see this kind of love in marriages. This love is unconditional, it does not love because it is receiving something from the other person Ephesians 5:25- [25] Husbands, love your wives, just as Christ loved the church and gave himself up for her.

This love is sacrificial, as Christ sacrificed his life for us; it goes the extra mile and does not care about what happens. It only cares about the happiness and joy the extra mile will give to the other person.

This love also forgives and forgets, does not refer to past mistakes or hurts as Christ's forgives us our sins each passing day.

Whiles we were yet sinners, Christ died for us Proverbs 10:12- [12] Hatred stirs up conflict, but love covers over all wrongs; Proverbs 17:9- [9] Whoever would foster love covers over an offense, but whoever repeats the matter separates close friend.   This love also trusts and makes sure it is easy for the other to trust them.

Agape love makes a woman submit and a husband love the wife as God has

~ 47 ~

instructed. It makes each other know they are not to take advantage or take each other's love for granted.

2. **Phileo**- *This is the brotherly love. The type of love you will show towards your family, brothers, sisters, brothers, etc. How you will treat them and what you will wish for them. That is what phileo love is about. That is the love you are supposed to demonstrate or show to each other Hebrews 13:1- 13 Keep on loving one another as brothers and sisters.*

This love binds siblings together and it must be shown in marriages.

This love plays, teases, respects and chats at all the times. This love is supportive and defends at all times. It gets angry alright, but yet still finds a way to play and get along again.

This love does not hit or abuse each other, it pampers and nourishes. Some people need to learn this kind of love, especially people that have had a bad upbringing; but agape love develops by the other person sacrificing, teaching and taking the other through it.

3. **Eros**- *Eros is the sexual love that creates intimacy between couples in marriage. It binds and brings them together.*

   Proverbs 5:19- [19] A loving doe, a graceful deer—may her breasts satisfy you always, may you ever be intoxicated with her love.

   It is the romance part of the marriage that has to be kept going at all times.

   This must not be stopped after the honeymoon. It must continue to avoid adultery. Couples must be able to talk about their sexual love, what they like to do, changes they would like and what tickles their fancy.

   Do not be ashamed to talk about it or go outside your marriage and try it somewhere. It should be adventurous and fun.

TRUST AND HONESTY

Trust is to have a belief in something and to believe that thing is good; to be able to wholly rely on something confidently.

It believes that a person will understand you, treat you well and will be responsible if you are with them.

This has to be the foundation for every relationship, the solid rock. Every relationship without trust cannot survive and work in the long run.

Trust is also been able to know the person you are with inside in and out. Being able to know at least most of their past. It is nearly impossible to really know someone completely before you live together—and even after in some cases.

Human beings are multifaceted creatures. Most people have multiple personalities; one for work, one for family and another for their sweetheart. Honesty forms part of trust.

It is the cornerstone of any healthy relationship and it breeds a bucketful of trust. Even telling the smallest untruths can destroy trust. Trust is the most basic element every marriage or relationship must have.

COMMITMENT AND PRIORITY

Commitment is the work, belief, loyalty that a person gives to a system. It is something that a person has to do regularly. This is also an important ingredient in every relationship and marriage.

Each person in the marriage has to be loyal, has to know the reason why they have decided to be in the marriage. Each person must know their obligation and be committed to make the marriage work, no matter what comes their way.

In marriage you have to be committed each day to the extent that you know it is part of your daily duties to make each other happy. Commitment means making up your mind to spend the rest of your life, day in and day out, with the same person. There are going to be times when things will turn upside down, but your commitment will keep you glued to this person for life. Especially when it comes to marriage, you make a vow and you must keep it.

Malachi 2:14-16-*14 You ask, "Why?" It is because the LORD is the witness between you and the wife of your youth. You have been unfaithful to her, though she is your partner; the wife of your marriage covenant.*

15 has not the one God made you? You belong to him in body and spirit. And what does the one God seek? Godly offspring. So be on your guard, and do not be unfaithful to the wife of your youth

16 "The man who hates and divorces his wife," says the LORD, the God of Israel, "does violence to the one he should protect says the LORD Almighty. So be on your guard, and do not be unfaithful.

Numbers 30:1-2- 30- Moses said to the heads of the tribes of Israel: "This is what the LORD commands: *² When a man makes a vow to the LORD or takes an oath to obligate himself by a pledge, he must not break his word but must do everything he said.*

The vow you make on the wedding day is not negotiable. It must be your priority to put your other half's happiness above everything else. You must have great organisational skills and be able to prioritise your life. You must learn to be faithful.

Corinthians 1, 4:2- *² Now it is required that those who have been given a trust must prove faithful.*

UNDERSTANDING

Couples, and a lot of other people, are together but do not understand each other or know they are a team. In every marriage or relationship there should not be a "hers" or a "his" team.

It must be one team because you both understand each others words, feelings and actions. You must understand the purpose of the relationship and why both of you the things you do do.

You are both from two different backgrounds, so you will see and do things differently. Differences can be charming; differences can be attractive. It depends on how you both use it to your advantage.

You need to be aware that each day will bring both good and bad. That is the nature of life.

The best way to prevent divorce is to acknowledge the vows you made and to understand that divorce is not an option. God calls on married couples to be understanding. Understanding also means being mature. Roman 15:5-6- *⁵ May the God who gives endurance and encouragement give you the same attitude of mind toward each other that Christ Jesus had, ⁶ so that with one mind and one voice you may glorify the God and Father of our Lord Jesus Christ.*

Understanding means listening and having a deeper connection of the mindset of the person you are with.

Sometimes it would have to be questions like "why" and "how" to understand the actions of each other and to live happily.

Do not be afraid to ask the why's and how's. If it will help you understand your partner better.

If your partner keeps asking, do not think they do not trust you, but use it as a learning curb for both of you to develop your knowledge about each other.

COMMUNICATION

One of the most difficult things is telling your partner how you feel. There are different types of communications, both verbal and non-verbal. Non-verbally describes actions and verbally describes words. Every successful relationship must have a good communication method.

The two types of communication must be used hand in hand for the success of the marriage. The bible encourages good communication in forms of speaking good words, positive words and to bring life into your marriage.

Proverbs 18:21- *[21]The tongue has the power of life and death, and those who love it will eat its fruit.*

You must learn to use loving words to nurture your marriage- Isaiah 50:4. *[4] The Sovereign LORD has given me a well-instructed tongue, to know the word that sustains the weary. He wakens me morning by morning, wakens my ear to listen like one being instructed;* Colossians 4:6- [6] *Let your conversation be always full of grace, seasoned with salt, so that you may know how to answer everyone* ; Proverbs 15:23 [23] *A person finds joy in giving an apt reply—and how good is a timely word!*

Communication results in growth. Ephesians 4:15- [15] *Instead, speaking the truth in love, we will grow to become in every respect the mature body of him who is the head, that is, Christ.*

Good communication is a critical component for a strong and healthy marriage; it can bring you together, closer than you can ever think, be it you live together or are miles apart.

Phone communications, emails, etc., are all forms of communication. Communication may also come in the form of gifts and presents to make each other feel appreciated.

The important aspect of being a communicator in a relationship is also being a good listener, not always wanting to be heard, but learning to hear your partner's point of view, ideas, worries and fears. You must let your thoughts die to have a peaceful marriage.

Good communication consists of sending and receiving of clear messages. If you communicate clearly, there will always be understanding and peace in the marriage.

If you are actively listening, you should not only be able to repeat what the other say, but you should also be able to communicate the feelings attached to it. More than half of all communications is non-verbal, with facial expressions, gestures, etc. You should be able to understand your partner's body language.

Listening is one of the best ways to show a person you care. Couples, who take time to really learn the act of listening, have the happiest, healthiest and most rewarding relationships.

CHAPTER 9
SEX

SEX

Job 31:1- I made a covenant with my eyes not to look lustfully at a young woman

1 John 2:15-17- 15 Do not love the world or anything in the world. If anyone loves the world, love for the Father is not in them. 16 For everything in the world—the lust of the flesh, the lust of the eyes, and the pride of life—comes not from the Father but from the world. 17 The world and its desires pass away, but whoever does the will of God lives forever.

In marriage, the Eros love is the sexual love. Sex is an important topic and subject in this century. Sex is no more regarded or respected.

The world brands sex as something you can go to a shop and buy. There are always advertisements of different sorts displaying and encouraging sex, especially within the youth.

The idea of sex and its value has been degraded. Some people even feel ashamed to talk about the fact that they are virgins these days.

Sex is part of God's creation and he created the feelings for it, but it must not be abused or taken for granted.

The main purpose God created sex has lost his great value all around the world. God created sex to be special, to be sacred; to be a bond, a unity, and an intimacy between two people, two souls who have decided to live their lives together, no matter what. It should be called love-making.

Sex is not just the releasing of hormones, semen and fluids; it is a connection, deeper than that what is done physically. It is a soul bond, physically, spiritually and emotionally. It is a soul tie, covenant through the releasing of the fluids between the two people.

This is why a creature can be made or formed through it. God made man in his own image; therefore, God could have given us the same advantage of creating another human through the way he created human. He made humans out of clay and breathed life into them, but in this case God instituted sex to make another human out of it. That shows how special God wants sex to be seen.

It can therefore be said that God's purpose for creating sex is mainly for reproduction and intimacy.

Intimacy is a sense of deeper feeling of belonging or affectionateness in a relationship.

Genesis 1:28- *28 God blessed them and said to them, "Be fruitful and increase in number; fill the earth and subdue it. Rule over the fish in the sea and the birds in the sky and over every living creature that moves on the ground."*

It is more than a physical union. It can be an avenue of transferring blessings or curses. It can bring favour and blessings if done under the right condition, at the right place and time. It can also bring regrets and barriers in life.

Once you become intimate with someone, you both become one flesh. If you have sex with different people, then you are fragmenting your life everywhere. You can protect yourself from sexually transmitted diseases, but you cannot protect yourself from sexually transmitted demons.

Most anointing has been denominated because of sex, because it has not been done under the right condition.

That is why God made sex for marriage. To avoid fornication, God advises everyone who wants to engage in the act to be married because he hates fornication, which most people do without guilt.

1 Corinthians 7:1- 2- *7 Now for the matters you wrote about: "It is good for a man not to have sexual relations with a woman. ² But since sexual immorality is occurring, each man should have sexual relations with his own wife, and each woman with her own husband."*

Sex or love-making is beautiful. It can be used for so many things. It is the highest expression of love; it is the most effective way of reconciliation. It can bring comforting or consoling to a partner. It can make a person feel special and appreciated, especially when it is done in marriage. It brings married people closer and gives them the inner belonging or sense of belonging, along with respect and dignity.

CHAPTER 10
BEING A HUSBAND

BEING A HUSBAND

Husband means "master of the house." It comes from an Old Norse word. As the master of the house, he binds or keeps a house together. That explains the role and duties of a husband.

- *You are to bind to keep your house together, no matter what. Being a husband is a great responsibility. You must know you are the head of the family, its coach, guide, protector and provider. You are also a source of security for your wife and children.*

  Ephesians 5:23- [23] For the husband is the head of the wife as Christ is the head of the church, his body, of which he is the Saviour.

- *You must also know that Christ is the head of the house and has put you in charge of it; therefore, if there is a problem, you must always go back to your source or father.*

  1 Corinthians 11:3- [3] But I want you to realize that the head of every man is

Christ, and the head of the woman is man and the head of Christ is God.

Ecclesiastes 9:9 ⁹ Enjoy life with your wife, whom you love, all the days of this meaningless life that God has given you under the sun—all your meaningless days. For this is your lot in life and in your toilsome labour under the sun.

- *You must be the spiritual leader of the house. When Adam and Eve sinned, God called Adam when he came to the garden. You must always be the one presenting your family to the Lord. You must be a provider.*

  1Timothy 5:8-. ⁸ Anyone who does not provide for their relatives, and especially for their own household, has denied the faith and is worse than an unbeliever.

- *You must also be aware that your wife is the neck. You must love your wife no matter what. Being the head does not mean taking decisions without your wife, or abusing her rights, imposing ideas on her and not understanding her. God made you the head because he knows the female or the wife is a weaker vessel and must be protected.*

Colossians 3:19- [19] *Husbands, love your wives and do not be harsh with them.*

- *You must make her feel happy at all the times and respect her. You must be a listener, a faithful friend who your wife could come to any time. You must be a motivator, have a vision and purpose in life. Importantly, you must be committed, disciplinarian and a selfless person who is able to sacrifice.*

- *You must be able to encourage your wife in the word of God and help her to organize her life. Through that you must learn to be very tolerant.*

1Peter 3:7 [7] *Husbands, in the same way be considerate as you live with your wives, and treat them with respect as the weaker partner and as heirs with you of the gracious gift of life, so that nothing will hinder your prayers.*

- *You must make her feel loved and wanted and accepted. Proverbs 5:18-* [18]

May your fountain be blessed, and may you rejoice in the wife of your youth.

- *You must nourish and cherish her.*

  Ephesians 5:25-29,—[25] Husbands, love your wives, just as Christ loved the church and gave himself up for her [26] to make her holy, cleansing her by the washing with water through the word, [27] and to present her to himself as a radiant church, without stain or wrinkle or any other blemish, but holy and blameless. [28] In this same way, husbands ought to love their wives as their own bodies. He who loves his wife loves himself. [29] After all, no one ever hated their own body, but they feed and care for their body, just as Christ does the church

- *Marriage rests on the shoulders of the man. He must know whatever happens in the home, it is his responsibility to bring peace, although it might not always be his fault. You must always be an apologetic person. You must be the source of the cleaving and always hold the marriage together because the head contains all the brains, arteries that control the body. God places the responsibility of cleaving on the man.*

Genesis 2:24- [24] That is why a man leaves his father and mother and is united to his wife, and they become one flesh

- *You must know and accept the feminine side of your wife, which may include excessive worrying and talking. That is part of how God created a woman; sometimes the talking becomes advice and if not listened to. Bad things may happen if you don't listen.*

CHAPTER 11
BEING A WIFE

BEING A WIFE

A wife is to be a helpmate, a supporter, motivator and a promoter. You must be virtuous. Proverbs 31:10-31 describes the role, duties and qualities of a wife-

[10] *A wife of noble character who can find? She is worth far more than rubies.* [11] *Her husband has full confidence in her and lacks nothing of value.* [12] *She brings him good, not harm, all the days of her life.* [13] *She selects wool and flax and works with eager hands.* [14] *She is like the merchant ships, bringing her food from afar.* [15] *She gets up while it is still night; she provides food for her family and portions for her female servants.* [16] *She considers a field and buys it; out of her earnings she plants a vineyard.* [17] *She sets about her work vigorously; her arms are strong for her tasks.* [18] *She sees that her trading is profitable, and her lamp does not go out at night.* [19] *In her hand she holds the distaff and grasps the spindle with her fingers.* [20] *She opens her arms to the poor and extends her hands to the needy.* [21] *When it snows, she has no fear for her household; for all of them are clothed in scarlet.* [22] *She makes coverings for her bed; she is clothed in fine linen and purple.* [23] *Her husband is respected at the city gate, where he*

*takes his seat among the elders of the land. [24]
She makes linen garments and sells them, and
supplies the merchants with sashes. [25] She is
clothed with strength and dignity; she can laugh
at the days to come. [26] She speaks with wisdom,
and faithful instruction is on her tongue. [27] She
watches over the affairs of her household
and does not eat the bread of idleness. [28] Her
children arise and call her blessed; her
husband also, and he praises her: [29] "Many
women do noble things, but you surpass them
all." [30] Charm is deceptive, and beauty is
fleeting; but a woman who fears the LORD is to
be praised. [31] Honour her for all that her hands
have done, and let her works bring her praise at
the city gate*

- You must learn to accept your husband
  the way he is and love him; this makes it
  easier for you to provide your marital
  duties as a wife. Always remember that
  he is the head and you are the neck.

  You must know how to turn the head
  towards the correct direction because if
  a head does not have a good or correct
  neck, it will not function and the whole
  body will suffer.

Titus 2:24-. ⁴ Then they can urge the younger women to love their husbands and children

- God made you as a helper. Helper means a supporter, an adviser and a prayer warrior. Gen 2:18, a companion

  You must be committed to the Lord - Proverbs 31:30- *³⁰ Charm is deceptive, and beauty is fleeting; but a woman who fears the LORD is to be praised.* You must be able to always go on your knees, be an intercessor and to support your family in prayers. This gives you a spirit of discernment, as the head may be busy with other things. .

- You must always submit. 1 Peter 3:1-6- *3 Wives, in the same way submit yourselves to your own husbands so that, if any of them do not believe the word, they may be won over without words by the behaviour of their wives, ² when they see the purity and reverence of your lives. ³ Your beauty should not come from outward adornment, such as elaborate hairstyles and the wearing of gold jewellery or fine clothes. ⁴ Rather, it should be that of your inner self, the* *unfading beauty of a gentle and quiet spirit, which is of great worth in God's sight. [5] For this is the way the holy women of the past who put their hope in God used to adorn themselves. They submitted themselves to their own husbands, [6] like Sarah, who obeyed Abraham and called him her lord. You are her daughters if you do what is right and do not give way to fear.*

Ephesians 5:22 [22] *Wives, submit yourselves to your own husbands as you do to the Lord.*

- You must be understanding and a friend to your husband. You must be ready to meet your husband's needs at all time, whether through intimacy or food preparation or dressing up to work or occasions

  Proverbs 21:9-. [9] *Better to live on a corner of the roof than share a house with a quarrelsome wife*

- You must be someone who he can rely on when he has a problem with the outside world. A friend also means being there and giving him words of encouragement not arguing with him all the time.

Proverbs 19:13- *13 A foolish child is a father's ruin, and a quarrelsome wife is like the constant dripping of a leaky roof*

You must be able to create a peaceful home, a welcoming home. You must be kind and committed. Proverbs 25:24- *24 Better to live on a corner of the roof than share a house with a quarrelsome wife.*

- You must be focused, have a vision or purpose in life to create a career Proverbs 31:27- *27 She watches over the affairs of her household and does not eat the bread of idleness.*

- An excellent home and housekeeper to keep your home clean and tidy at all times. You must be reliable, be a hostess, hospitable because you will have in-laws, friends and family coming over. You must know what your roles are and accept your roles. You must know how to make your husband happy. Titus 2:4-5. *4 Then they can urge the younger women to love their husbands and children, 5 to be self-controlled and pure, to be busy at home, to be kind, and to be subject to their husbands, so that no one will malign the word of God*

- You must be patient and loving

CHAPTER 12
MARRIAGE IN THIS CENTURY

MARRIAGE IN THIS CENTURY

There are a lot of controversies about the roles of husbands and wives in today's 21st century.

Back in the day, women belonged to the kitchen and had the role of staying home, being housewives and looking after the children; whereas the men went out to look for greener pastures to feed the family.

A good marriage will start with the ideal and support of what the bible says the roles, responsibilities, and qualities of husbands and wives are; but in this age and time, it is difficult to follow them all.

Nowadays, things have all but changed and it makes marriage more difficult. Many women have careers and they go to work to help look after the family. This has brought the idea of equality between husbands and wives.

The Bible still supports headship, but in this world what does that mean and how do couples apply it when both husbands and wives are the breadwinners of the family?

The bible does not provide a platform for husbands to abuse their wives.

For example, some husbands will make all the decisions in the world and will not give the wife the chance to input.

They will support their decisions with a bible quote: "The Bible says the husband is the head." This is wrong. One thing God hates and takes seriously, is abuse.

The marriage has to be a partnership, with equality status. Yet, both husbands and wives knowing how they fit in to create the perfect atmosphere they want at home.

It all goes back to being submissive to each other, understanding your roles and making decisions together.

It also means implementing the basic ingredients for a good marriage. If both of you understand each other and know you are partners, it makes the marriage an easy one. For example, a husband can do the shopping and a wife can as well.

When a husband gets home early, he can cook the dinner and the wife can wash up the dishes after.

Just because the Bible says the wife should be the housekeeper doesn't mean she should do all the housework like cooking, cleaning, shopping, etc.

These important roles must be agreed upon and decided on based on what both of you want and do for a living.

Careers are important as well. Couples need to decide whose career will take the precedence.

Importantly, there are many questions that need to be asked, so couples in this century need to sit down and agree on before them before they walk down the aisle to say *I do*. Questions like:

1. *Do you both have the same views on gender roles?*

2. *Are you both comfortable with ambitions?*

3. *Where are both of you going to live after the wedding?*

4. *What roles will family and friends have in your marriage?*

5. *What are your household priorities?*

6. *Whose responsibility is what? E.g. cooking, shopping, cleaning, ironing, etc.*

7. *How will you divide household chores?*

8. *Who will manage the finances and what will your financial goals be? Do you both want joint accounts and separate accounts? Who will manage the debts and pay bills like the mortgage or rent, etc?*

9. *What are your future goals?*

10. *Do you both share the same views on children? Whether their upbringing or when to have them?*

11. *How will you manage conflict?*

12. *What are the effective ways to avoid arguing in the marriage?*

There should always be a way of resolving conflicts in the marriage, especially when one person's role is lacking. For example, if the husband is not managing the finances well, the wife must be given the opportunity to manage them. .

Another example, if the wife is a bad cook, the husband must understand and take that role of cooking to help. The responsibilities in the marriage must not be one-way traffic; it must go both ways.

Couples should always remember they are in partnership and learn to manage conflicts.

CHAPTER 13
DIVORCE PROOF YOUR MARRIAGE

DIVORCE PROOF YOUR MARRIAGE

No one gets married to divorce and divorce should not be an option, but when it happens there is nothing that can be done about it

1 Corinthians 7:10-11- *[10] To the married I give this command (not I, but the Lord): A wife must not separate from her husband. [11] But if she does, she must remain unmarried or else be reconciled to her husband. And a husband must not divorce his wife.*

Mark 10:9 -*[9] therefore what God has joined together, let no one separate."*

It causes so many problems like low self-esteem, step-children etc. Before you take your vows, you must know that you are making a covenant with this person, not just with this person but with God. God takes covenants very seriously and once one is broken, he deals with it-

Ecclesiastes 5:4- 5 *[4] When you make a vow to God, do not delay to fulfil it. He has no pleasure*

in fools; fulfil your vow. ⁵ It is better not to make a vow than to make one and not fulfil it.

Malachi 2:14-16-¹⁴ *You ask, "Why?" It is because the LORD is the witness between you and the wife of your youth. You have been unfaithful to her, though she is your partner; the wife of your marriage covenant.¹⁵ has not the one God made you? You belong to him in body and spirit. And what does the one God seek? Godly offspring. So be on your guard, and do not be unfaithful to the wife of your youth ¹⁶ "The man who hates and divorces his wife," says the LORD, the God of Israel, "does violence to the one he should protect," says the LORD Almighty. So be on your guard, and do not be unfaithful.*

Have you ever wondered why the wedding ring is round? It has no end, it's a circle, you can go round and round in it; you cannot get out of it. That is the picture you must have in your head before you decide to put that on. Take the ring as a room you have been in, an enclosed room with no doors, no windows to escape, but within the room you have been given the basic needs of survival.

What do you do when there is a problem, or you find you need to do something? You work with the things that have been given to you in the room, to make food, fire to warm yourself and a bed to lay your head.

You may also see it from this angle: If you were put in a desert, you still have to eat, drink, keep warm and sleep. What do you do?

You find wood and stones and try making fire to keep warm and to cook something to eat. That must be the most important and most vital information you must have in the back of your head.

When you have put that ring on and announced to the whole world "for better; for worse, for richer, for poorer," you must learn to survive by those words.

Do you know the meaning of MRS? It only means M- My, R-Real, S-Sister. The man must love his real sister. Do not give the devil a chance to drop ideas in your head to destroy your marriage. John 10:*10-10* the *thief comes only to steal and kill and destroy; I have come that they may have life, and have it to the fullest.*

WAYS TO DIVORCE PROOF YOUR MARRIAGE

There were things that attracted you both to each other, things that you both saw and liked. Those things must be nourished or kept after the marriage to divorce proof the marriage.

Most people get complacent, relaxed and stop doing the things that kept them going during the courtship period. Why? It's because they are married now.

The most successful marriages are the ones that have a lot of activities, a lot of adventures, a lot of different things going on. It makes the marriage exciting and stops each other from saying they are bored or he/she has changed. Things like, "He is not the same person I married or she is not the same person I married.

She does not dress that way anymore or he does not talk to me the way he used to before." Always bring the vibe and keep the fire going in your relationship.

- *If your wife loved you to call her 24/7 at work, do not stop doing it because you have placed the ring on her finger.*

- *If your husband loved to see you wear all the sexiest lingerie on earth, buy more to wear and show him. Make your marriage life enjoyable. If you do not do so, someone else will give him/her the attention and he/she might run to the arms of another person. Learn to divorce proof your marriage.*

- *Go on romantic dinners, do not stay home and eat the same foods all the time. Surprise your spouse with a nicely cooked meal when she is back from work, especially if she normally does the cooking. A nice treat, a soak in the bath after and a nice massage. Women loves attention*

- *Plan a surprise break away or vacation. Some couples have not taken a holiday together since they have been married. Book time off from work. Change of environment does a great lot in our lives. Re-kindle the love by experiencing something new somewhere else apart from the four corners of your house.*

- *If your spouse loves going to the movies or pictures, make it a habit to know which thriller he/she enjoys most. Get him/her a surprise ticket to watch the new movie that has just come out with his/her best actor/actress in it.*

Above all, and most importantly, love each other as you want to be loved; love each other as God wants you to love each other; know divorce is not an option, and always go back to your daily BIBLE for every problem you face.

Learn to communicate effectively with each other, understand each other, instead of going to the world for solutions for your problems in your marriage. Learn to talk to the author of every marriage, God, and seek his intervention and advice. Learn to divorce proof your marriage; know divorce is not an option.

Learn to pray and worship with your spouse always and have a blessed marriage life!

TRUE MEANING OF LOVE

If it's because of his eyes or his lips or his great body; it's not love....... It's lust

If it's because of his intelligence or insight about life; it's not love..... It's admiration

If it's because he cries every time you try to leave; it's not love..... It's pity

If it's because he makes you forget to study and sleep; it's not love... It's infatuation

Love is when you do not know why you seem to be attracted to this person.

Love has its reason and the reason is UNKNOWN.

MARRIAGE

M – Marriage binds two people in body and mind

A – And allows them to appreciate the miracles they find

R – Romance and compassion carry them along

R – Respect and acceptance make the marriage strong

I – Imparting words and actions of love from deep inside

A – Acknowledging each other while standing side by side

G – Great marriages are created by husbands and wives

E – Eternally being grateful they are in each other's lives